UPRIGHT

OLD *GLORY*

by
Adriane L. Johnson

Dedication

I dedicate *Upright Old Glory* to all of the patriots: the brave men and women who have made the ultimate sacrifice and those who are currently serving our nation. I express my gratitude and admiration for their commitment to the United States of America – to preserving our Democracy, our freedoms and our way of life.

I also dedicate this book to the current freedom fighters – those who are pushing back and ensuring that our Democracy is intact for generations to come. You are true patriots, and you are an inspiration to all.

Acknowledgement

Writing *Upright Old* Glory was a cathartic moment, a way of expressing my raw emotions about recent accounts of high-level officials flying the U.S. flag upside down as an act of defiance.

Upright Old Glory embodies the spirit of patriotism and relates to acknowledging the sacrifices and actions of men and women who serve and have served in the armed forces.

Upright Old Glory is a tribute to the unwavering spirit of patriotism that everyday Americans embody. May this poem reflect the strength and resilience represented by the flag that we all must protect.

Let us forever remember our brothers and sisters, who laid down their lives for our peace and our freedom. To our heroes everywhere. *Upright Old Glory* is dedicated to those who pass the staff of freedom's waving shield.

I want to thank my husband, Bruce, and my daughter, Nia their unwavering love and support! And finally, I want to thank Letitia Anderson and Allison Richard for inspiring me to share *Upright Old Glory* with the World!

About the Author

Adriane Johnson is a public servant, an entrepreneur, an aspiring poet and author.   She consistently solves complex problems by advancing meaningful legislation, helps people who are most vulnerable, and makes a positive impact in the communities that she serves.

I am the flag of the United States of America - respect me!

My name is Old Glory - recognize me

Upside down you display me

Inverting Old Glory you disrespect me

Ignoring institutional values is clear to see that
anarchy is part of your strategy

Protesting freedom and equality for all

Creating a wilderness of mirrors in a hail storm

Infringing on women's bodily autonomy with the
Supreme Court backing and far-right wing ideology

Attempting to dismantle our Constitution,

Our Democracy, and our inalienable rights

Browning of America and the globe is the accelerant driving this misguided and hate-fueled fight

Desecrating a world-renowned symbol of unity

Trying to hijack our nation just to appease a wannabe deity

Changing the flag's upright stature

Not because of an incursion, wartime or distress

Undermining our legal system, supporting Satan
incarnate even in light of his impending arrest

Twisting the truth about our rich history
Condemning our Military heroes and making a
mockery out of the land of opportunity

Upright Old Glory will always prevail

Working through yet another rocky SEASON

Praying to God almighty to unveil the REASON

Why it feels like it will take a LIFETIME to change the hearts of the Third Position to see that

Dishonoring those who fought and made the ultimate sacrifice to protect

all Americans' way of life

will only bring on generational strife

Flying Old Glory upright

is in the flag code

shining a spotlight on our nation's symbol of
strength, justice and freedom

must be told

from the mountaintop

Upright is the way to display

and fly Old Glory

From land to sea

to the shining sea to the bounds

of our solar system in perpetuity

Upright Old Glory is mighty good to see!